THE AMAZING ECUADORIAN COOKBOOK

Amazing Ecuatorian Recipes

Camila Navia

Supernova Star Books

CONTENTS

INTRODUCTION

Ecuadorian food is a mixture of indigenous, African and Spanish influences. It is known for its spicy dishes and its use of fresh, local ingredients, such as potatoes, corn, yucca and plantains. Fish and seafood dishes are also common, as Ecuador is a coastal country.

Its gastronomy is a mixture of indigenous, African and Spanish influences. In addition, Ecuadorian food also includes a variety of vegetarian dishes, such as "locro de papas", a potato and vegetable soup, and "empanadas de viento", empanadas stuffed with cheese and vegetables.

The style of cuisine varies according to the region of the country. On the coast, the food is spicier and is based on the use of seafood, such as fish and shellfish. One of the most popular dishes on the coast is "ceviche". It is also common to find dishes based on shrimp and prawns, such as "encocado de camarones" and "langostinos al coco".

In the Sierra, the food is more traditional and is based on the use of products of the region, such as potatoes, corn and yucca. One of the most popular dishes in the Sierra is "choclo con queso", which is a tamale made with cooked corn and stuffed with cheese. It is also common to find meat-based dishes, such as "llapingacho", a kind of potato tortilla filled with minced and cooked meat, and "churrasco", which is a grilled meat dish served with rice and vegetables.

If you want to enjoy a unique and delicious culinary experience, don't hesitate to try the food of Ecuador! We promise you won't regret it.

BREAKFAST

GREEN PLANTAIN EMPANADAS WITH CHEESE

Preparation time: 30 minutes
Servings: 4
Ingredients:
3 green plantains
Cheese to taste
Salt to taste

Recommended materials:

- Empanada mold: **https://amzn.to/3Vo6JDK**

Preparation: In a pot with water and salt we boil the greens until they are soft. Without letting them cool, drain the greens and with the help of a rolling pin we crush them very well, in this process we must add the butter and form a very thin and homogeneous dough. When the dough is ready we are going to form medium sized balls, we stretch the plastic wrap and place the green balls on it and cover it with another layer of plastic wrap, with the help of the rolling pin we stretch the dough as much as possible, until it is in a circular shape. Add the grated fresh cheese right in the middle of the circle and close it. With the help of a round soup bowl cut the edges so that the empanadas are perfect, so that the empanada is completely closed we can crush the edges with a fork.

Heat enough oil in a frying pan to cover the empanadas and fry them until they are golden brown and crispy on both sides.

PATACONES

Preparation time: 1 hour
Servings: 4
Ingredients:
4 green plantains
Frying oil
Salt to taste

Recommended materials:

- Pataconera: https://amzn.to/3hR3yXk

Preparation: Peel the plantains and cut them into thick slices, you can make straight or diagonal cuts. Heat the oil over medium heat in a frying pan, the amount of oil should cover the slices. Fry the plantains until they start to turn yellow without letting them brown. Remove the slices from the pan and crush with a rolling pin-like utensil known as a pataconera, you can also use a mortar or the bottom of a glass. Fry again for approximately 2 minutes until they are completely golden brown and crispy. Remove the tostones from the pan and add more salt if necessary. Serve the patacones with queso fresco.

BOLON WITH CHEESE AND CHICHARRON

Preparation time: 45 minutes
Servings: 4
Ingredients:
2 green plantains
150 grams of pork cracklings
150 grams of white or fresh cheese
½ dessert spoon of salt
1 tablespoon of butter
Frying oil

Preparation: Remove the plantains peel and cut them in half. In this step, you can choose the cooking method you prefer. We decided to boil them. It takes about 15 minutes for them to be ready, if you count from the moment it starts boiling. When they are cooked, drain them and knead them with the help of a pestle. Add the salt and the tablespoon of butter. When it is still warm, at least enough to handle with your hands, add the finely chopped or ground pork rinds and the coarsely grated cheese. Mix everything very well, knead it with your hands until it is integrated. Form the dumplings with your hands to give them a rounded shape.

*It is not necessary to fry the dough if you want to take care of your diet, if so, cook the pork rinds separately and then add them to the plantain dough together with the other ingredients.

Fry the plantain balls in plenty of hot oil. Make sure they are browned on all sides. Let them dry on paper to absorb the excess fat.

MOTE PILLO

Preparation time: 25 minutes
Servings: 4
Ingredients:
4 cups of cooked mote
2 tablespoons butter
¼ chopped white onion
8 Eggs
½ teaspoon of salt
1 Cup Milk
Preparation: In a frying pan fry butter, onion and salt. Add the eggs and then the mote, mix well and cook. When the eggs are cooked add the milk without letting it dry too much, for a good flavor the key is that the mote gets wet with the milk, if it dries add more milk. Serve with spices to taste.

YUCA BREAD

Preparation time: approximately 2 hours
Portions: 20 loaves
Ingredients:
2 ½ cups cassava starch
4 cups grated cheese
1 teaspoon baking powder
1 pinch of salt
4 ounces of butter
2 eggs
3 tablespoons of water or milk (if the dough is dry)

Preparation:
Preheat the oven to 500F. Mix the cassava starch, cheese, baking powder, salt and knead well. Add the butter and eggs and continue kneading for 5 minutes until the mixture is smooth and homogeneous. If it is dry, add a little water or milk to soften.
Form the loaves into small balls and place them on a greased tray.
Bake for approximately 7 minutes and turn on the oven broiler until the breads are golden brown, approximately 3-5 minutes. Serve the yuca breads warm.

TIGRILLO DE VERDE

Preparation time: 30m
Servings: 4
Ingredients:
2 green plantains
2 tablespoons of oil or butter
1 onion
1 tomato
200 grams of mozzarella cheese
200 grams of pork rinds
4 eggs
1 pinch of salt to taste

Preparation:
Choose large green plantains, as this is the only way to get a good green tigrillo. Remove the peel from the green plantains and cut them into more or less large pieces. Fry the plantain pieces in abundant oil or boil them. Once fried or boiled, grind the plantain pieces. It is not necessary to make a puree. Fry the onion and tomato in butter. Add the mashed plantain, cheese, chicharrón and eggs. Stir the ingredients in the pan. Finish frying the ingredients when the chicharrón and egg are fried.

If you wish, add a fried egg to enjoy the tigrillo mixed with the egg yolk.

Tigrillo can also be served with stew.

APPETIZERS

ECUADORIAN CEVICHE OF FISH

Preparation time: 75m
Servings: 8
Ingredients:
1 Kilo albacore tuna
20 to 30 Lemons
Salt to taste
Pepper to taste
Bunch of coriander
3 red onions cut in cubes
1 tomato
½ tablespoon mustard

Preparation: Chop the fish into small cubes. Place the fish pieces in a bowl. Squeeze the lemons and add the juice to the bowl where the fish is, the juice should cover all the fish. Let the fish rest in the lemon for an hour, until it cures, in the open air it takes an hour, in refrigeration it usually takes longer. Add the onion and half of the diced tomato, without the seeds, to the bowl. Add salt and pepper to taste, mix well. Add the cilantro and the tablespoon of mustard and mix very well, the acid to be absorbed by the fish is reduced, add lemon to taste if you are looking for acidity. Add half a liter of water to the bowl.
Let it cool in the refrigerator for 15 minutes before consuming. Enjoy with white rice, popcorn and chifles.

Recommendations:
It is best to reserve the fish in lemon a day in advance to save time.

SHRIMP CEVICHE

Preparation time: 75m
Servings: 8
Ingredients:
1 Kilo of shrimp
2 red onions
2 ripe tomatoes
2 green or red peppers
1 bunch of cilantro or coriander
Juice of 5 lemons
1 tablespoon mustard
½ cup tomato sauce or tomato juice
2 tablespoons of oil
Salt and pepper to taste

Preparation: Place the shrimp in a pot of boiling salted water and boil for 5 minutes. Strain the shrimp and let them cool in water with ice cubes to stop cooking immediately.

Peel the onion and cut it into thin half-moons. Rinse the pieces in water and salt. Peel the tomatoes, remove the seeds and cut into cubes. Cut the peppers into cubes. Mix the onion, tomatoes and peppers with the tomato sauce, mustard, chopped coriander, salt, pepper and oil. When the shrimp are cold, place them in the previous mixture. Let stand in the refrigerator for approximately 2 hours.

Serve the ceviche with patacones, chifles or popcorn.

CEVICHE OF CHOCHO (TARWI)

Preparation time: 30 minutes
Servings: 8
Ingredients:
4 cups of cooked chochos
Juice of 10 lemons
Juice of 2 oranges
1 red onion cut in thin slices
3 Tomatoes cut in cubes
1 bunch of coriander, finely chopped
½ cup tomato sauce or juice
2 tablespoons olive oil
Salt to taste

Preparation: Place the red onion in a bowl, sprinkle with salt and cover with warm water. Let soak for 10 minutes, strain the water and rinse the onions with cold water. Mix the onions, tomatoes, chochos, tomato sauce, cilantro, lime juice, orange juice, oil and salt. Marinate the ceviche for a couple of hours in the refrigerator. Serve the ceviche well chilled with chulpi (roasted corn), chifles, avocado or aji criollo.

CHIFLES

Preparation time: 30 minutes
Servings: 4
Ingredients:
4 Green plantains
Oil
Salt to taste

Preparation:
Place the oil in a frying pan and heat it over high heat for about 5 minutes. Peel the plantains and cut them into thin slices. Fry the slices until golden brown on both sides. Remove the plantains and leave them on absorbent paper. Sprinkle it with sea salt and serve hot. They can be served with cheese.

CORN WITH CHEESE SAUCE

Preparation time: 30 minutes
Servings: 4
Ingredients:
4 corn
½ cup cilantro
3 crushed garlic
1 cup milk
1 cup cheese
Water
Salt to taste

Preparation: First boil the corn, add salt to the water and add the 4 corn. Boil for 20 minutes until they are soft. In the blender add the bunch of coriander, the garlic, the cup of milk, salt to taste and the cheese. Blend very well. Once ready, add it on top of the corn and we can enjoy and serve.

CHEESE FINGERS

Preparation time: 30 minutes
Servings: 6
Ingredients:
1 Lb of Flour
1 tablespoon of salt
2 tablespoons sugar
1 cup butter
½ Lb cheese
1 cup of water
Oil

Preparation: Prepare the dough in a large bowl with the flour, salt, sugar and butter. Unite and mix the ingredients well until a homogeneous mixture is obtained. Add cold water and knead until the mixture is not sticky and is compact. Spread the dough with a mallet on a flat, clean and previously floured surface. Spread the dough until it is about 3 millimeters thick and cut it into strips of approximately 2 centimeters. Once the dough is ready, cut the cheese. Use a white cheese, of hard consistency and preferably salty. Take a piece of cheese and turn it with the dough until it is covered, in the shape of a screw or spiral. It is very important not to leave any piece uncovered.

Fry in a frying pan with very hot oil until the dough is golden brown. Remember to control the heat so that the pieces do not burn too quickly.

When removed, place on absorbent paper to remove excess oil.

SALADS

SALCHIPAPAS

Preparation time: 1 hour
Servings: 4
Ingredients:
4 or 5 large potatoes
4 Sausages
Frying oil
Salt to taste

Preparation: Peel and cut the potatoes into thick strips and soak them in cold water for half an hour. Drain the water and dry the potatoes well. Heat the frying oil to 325 F. Place the potatoes in the boiling oil and cook until tender, but not browned. Remove the potatoes from the oil and place them on paper towels to drain the oil. Let them cool for at least one hour. Reheat the oil again, this time to 375 F. Place the potatoes in the boiling oil and fry until golden brown and crispy.
Cut the sausages in half, with a cross cut at the ends and fry them. Place the potatoes and sausages on paper towels to remove the grease and serve immediately accompanied with pink sauce and tomato and onion curtido.

Preparation: In a saucepan of boiling water over medium heat, and cook the potatoes for 8 minutes, when soft, drain and set aside until cold. In a bowl, place the previously cooked and cold potatoes. Add the peas, chopped and cooked carrots and mayonnaise. Mix all the ingredients well, being careful not to crush the potatoes and peas. Add a little salt and pepper.

RUSSIAN SALAD

Preparation time: 18 minutes
Servings: 6
Ingredients:
5 Potatoes, peeled and diced
¼ cup peas
¼ cup mayonnaise
2 cups water
¼ cup carrot, diced small and cooked

POTATO SALAD WITH TUNA

Preparation time: 18 minutes
Servings: 2
Ingredients:
4 Potatoes
1 piece of onion
2 Cans of Tuna
2 tablespoons of Mayonnaise
Salt to taste

Preparation: Wash and peel the potatoes and then cut them into medium-sized cubes. Cook them in boiling water until slightly soft. Drain and set aside. It is important not to cut the potato too small because it could be mashed and we do not want that. On the other hand, while we let the potatoes cool down to room temperature, add the tuna, mayonnaise and diced onion, and mix them in a bowl with the potatoes. Mash everything until a tuna paste is formed, check the seasoning and add salt and pepper to taste.

TOMATO AND ONION CURTIDO

Preparation time: 20 minutes
Servings: 4
Ingredients:
3 tomatoes
2 Red Onions
2 Lemons
Cilantro
Salt

Preparation: Cut the onion and tomato in julienne strips. Cut the Cilantro leaves. Place onion in a bowl with lemon juice. Let macerate for about 10 minutes. Add tomato and cilantro, add salt to taste.

BEET SALAD

Preparation time: 40 minutes
Servings: 4
Ingredients:
Cooked beets
3 potatoes
1 can of peas
3 carrots
2 hard-boiled eggs
Homemade mayonnaise
Salt

Preparation: Peel the potatoes and cut them into medium-sized cubes. Peel the carrots and cut them into thin slices. Place both vegetables in a pot with water and cook for 20 minutes or until the ingredients are tender. Once ready, remove, drain and let cool in the refrigerator. When the potato salad is cold, remove it and mix it with the cooked and diced beets, the chopped hard-boiled eggs and the drained peas. Add mayonnaise to taste.

SOUPS

LOCRO OF POTATO

Preparation time: 1 hour
Servings: 8
Ingredients:
10 potatoes, peeled and cut into large chunks
2 tablespoons oil or butter
1 onion, diced
2 cloves garlic, finely chopped
2 teaspoons cumin
1 or 2 teaspoons of ground annatto
7 cups of water
1 cup milk
1 cup grated or shredded cheese
4 tablespoons finely chopped cilantro
Salt to taste

Preparation: Heat the oil or butter over medium heat in a pot and add the onion, garlic, cumin and ground achiote. Cook for 5 minutes until the onions are soft. Add the potatoes to the pot, mix well and continue cooking for about 5 minutes. Add the water and boil until the potatoes are tender. Mash the potatoes, but not all of them. The consistency of the locro should be creamy, but with small pieces of potato. Reduce the temperature, add the milk, mix well and cook for an additional 5 minutes. Add more milk or water if the soup is too thick. Add salt to taste, cheese and cilantro. Serve the locro de papas hot with avocados.

ENCEBOLLADO

Preparation time: 1 hour
Servings: 4
Ingredients:
1 kg of albacore (Tuna fillet)
1 green bell pepper
½ cup celery
1 ½ kg cassava
½ teaspoon cumin
750 gr of onion
1 medium onion
2 medium tomatoes
2 cloves garlic
2 tablespoons chili
½ tablespoon cumin
Cilantro and parsley to taste
Basil

Preparation: In a pot with water we place yucca with salt. Let it cook, in a separate pot put 2 liters of water, add the celery, tomatoes, medium onion, cilantro, parsley, crushed garlic, salt and pepper to taste. Stir and add the albacore. Cover and let it boil. Then blend one cup of yucca with one cup of water where the yucca was cooked and set aside. After 10 minutes. We take out the Albacora and the rest we leave covered so that it continues cooking for 30 minutes more. We let the time pass and take out the vegetables and the vegetables. We put it in a blender with some of the broth and blend it. After this we put it back in the pot, together with the yucca that was liquefied. Mix well and let it cook for 5 more minutes. Then in another saucepan put the onion previously washed and chopped, add cilantro, 3 tablespoons of oil and the juice of 6 lemons. Stir well. Serve the plates with the broth, the albacore and the encebollado salad on top.

AGUADO DE GALLINA

Preparation time: 2 hours
Servings: 6
Ingredients:
1 kilo of hen prey
¾ cup uncooked rice
2 tablespoons oil or butter
1 red onion, diced
1 bell pepper cut in cubes
6 crushed garlic cloves
2 tablespoons parsley, finely chopped
1 teaspoon dried oregano
1 teaspoon ground cumin
1 teaspoon ground annatto
8 cups of water
2 potatoes, peeled and cut into chunks
1 cup diced carrots
2 tablespoons finely chopped cilantro
Salt and pepper to taste

Preparation: Soak the rice in water for 30 minutes. Heat the oil or butter in a large pot and add the onion, garlic, bell bell pepper, parsley, oregano, cumin, achiote, salt and pepper. Cook for 10 minutes, stirring frequently. Add the water and wait until it boils. Add the chicken and cook over medium heat for 30 minutes. Add the soaked rice and potatoes. Cook for 45 minutes over low heat, stirring occasionally. Add the carrots and cook for 10 minutes until tender. Remove from the heat and add the cilantro. Serve the aguado with avocado and chili.

REPE DE LOJA

Preparation time: 2 hours
Servings: 6
Ingredients:
6 green plantains
1 onion, diced
200 gr of lojano cheese
75 ml of milk cream
1500 ml of water
2 tablespoons oil
2 crushed garlic cloves
Fresh cilantro
Salt

Preparation: Start by frying the onion and chopped garlic in a preheated pan with oil. Once they are golden brown, add the water. When it comes to a boil add the diced plantain and cook over low heat for half an hour. Slightly mix the vegetables to thicken the preparation, add the lojano cheese together with the milk and add salt to taste. Serve the repe with fresh cilantro.

RASPADO DE VERDE

Preparation time: 1 hour
Servings: 4
Ingredients:
3 green plantains
2 liters of water
1 egg
½ lb cheese
½ liter of milk
1 sprig of white onion
Ground garlic
Oregano
Butter
Salt and coriander to taste

Preparation: Make a stir-fry of chopped white onion, garlic, butter and oregano. Boil the water together with the refried mixture for 10 minutes. Scrape the plantain with a table spoon and add to the boiling water, cook for 15 minutes.

Add the cheese, milk and cilantro and leave for 5 minutes. Beat the egg yolk with a little of the soup liquid and then add it.

MENESTRÓN

Preparation time: 2 hours
Servings: 4
Ingredients:
2 cups of dried beans
½ lb of diced beef
½ pearl onion cut into cubes
½ diced bell bell pepper
1 carrot cut in cubes
2 crushed garlic seeds
2 tablespoons chopped fresh basil
1 tablespoon achiote
1 cup penne noodles
2 large potatoes cut in 4 pieces

Preparation: Soak the beans the day before. Make the sauce with the garlic, onion, bell pepper, basil and achiote, let it cool to room temperature and then blend it. Place the result of the refried mixture in the pot where the broth is going to be made, put a liter and a half of water to boil. Put the meat in the pot together with the beans when the water has boiled, let it boil for one hour. Add the noodles, potatoes and carrots.

Verify that the noodles and potatoes are well cooked and add the cheese and let it cook for a few minutes. Remove from heat and serve hot.

CHARD CREAM

Preparation time: 2 hours
Servings: 4
Ingredients:
Handful of chard
3 tablespoons butter
2 cups of milk
3 cloves garlic
½ onion
Cheese to taste
Oil
Salt and pepper to taste

Preparation:
Put water in a pot and then the well-washed chard. Let it boil for three minutes. After 3 minutes. Remove the chard and drain well. Then put them in the blender and add the cheese, in small pieces, the onion, milk, garlic, salt and pepper to taste.
Blend, to make the cream. Then in a pot we add butter and when it gets a little hot we add the blended cream and cook, let it boil for about 3 minutes and that's it!

CHUPÉ DE PESCADO

Preparation time: 2 hours
Servings: 6
Ingredients:
2 lb of filleted fish
2 lb of chola potato
1 cup milk
½ lb cheese
1 ear of corn on the cob
1 cup of beans
¼ cup vegetable oil
1 teaspoon achiote
1 branch of white onion
1 sprig of coriander
2 tablespoons garlic seasoning
1 tablespoon butter
1 cup flour
1 cabbage leaf
½ carrot
½ bell pepper
Salt and pepper to taste

Preparation:
Dice the carrot and finely chop the white onion. Cut the corn cob in pieces and the tail in small pieces. Fry the white onion with achiote, butter and half a spoonful of garlic, together with 2 diced potatoes. Add a liter and a half of water when the white onion is transparent. Chop the rest of the potatoes into larger cubes so that they do not fall apart and add them to the soup together with the carrot. Season the fish with garlic and salt to taste. Coat in flour and fry in a frying pan with oil until golden brown. Add the fried fish to the soup along with the cabbage, cheese, milk, coriander and a slice of bell pepper. Add salt to taste and serve.

YAHUARLOCRO

Preparation time: 2 hours
Servings: 6
Ingredients:
Lamb offal (belly, tripe or tripe giblets)
1 liter of fresh lamb blood
2 kilos of potatoes, peeled and cut into cubes
2 onions, finely chopped
2 tablespoons finely chopped cilantro
1 tablespoon oregano
1 tablespoon ground cumin
1 crushed garlic clove
4 tablespoons oil
4 ounces of liquefied peanuts dissolved in a cup with milk
1 teaspoon ground annatto
2 tablespoons parsley, finely chopped
2 lemons
Leaves of good grass
Salt and pepper to taste

Preparation: Wash the menudo with abundant water, then add 2 tablespoons of salt, the juice of the lemons and the hierbabuena leaves. Squeeze the whole menudo until the yellowish film that covers it comes out. Let it rest for a few minutes and wash it again with cold water. Place the menudo in a pressure cooker, add enough water and cook until tender. Remove the giblets from the broth and chop it finely. Heat 2 tablespoons of oil in a large pot and add the achiote, one chopped onion, coriander, cumin, pepper and garlic. Cook for 5 minutes. Add the potatoes and the peanuts dissolved in the milk, cover and boil for 15 minutes. Add the broth from the menudo and let the potatoes cook well. Before removing the pot from the fire add the chopped menudo. Separately, place the blood in a pot with 2 liters of boiling water and salt. Cook for 30 minutes. Remove from the fire and strain the water. Place the cooked blood in a flat dish and crumble it with your fingers, taking care to remove all impurities. Heat the oil in a frying pan and add the blood, pepper, parsley and a chopped onion. Fry well until the blood is fried. Serve the yahuarlocro very hot with the blood on top accompanied by a slice of avocado, a slice of tomato and pickled onion.

LENTIL SOUP

Preparation time: 2 hours
Servings: 6
Ingredients:
3 potatoes cut in cubes
400 gr of lentils
250 gr of Ecuadorian cheese
1 tablespoon butter
½ liter of milk
1 cup soup noodles
1 pearl onion
1 green bell pepper
3 cloves garlic
1 teaspoon basil
1 teaspoon achiote oil
Salt taste

Preparation: Soak the lentils in water for one hour. Heat a pot with the lentils and the water where they were soaked. In a blender, blend the bell pepper, garlic and onion with a little water. Incorporate it to the pot with the lentils and add the achiote and the potatoes. Cook until they soften. Add the noodles with about two cups of water and the fresh basil. Cook until the noodles soften and adjust the flavor. Finally, add the oregano, butter, milk and cheese, and wait about 5 minutes to remove from the heat. Serve hot and enjoy.

NOODLE SOUP WITH CHEESE

Preparation time: 30 minutes
Servings: 8
Ingredients:
1 cup whole milk
7 ounces of noodles
1 lb of peeled potatoes in squares
2 tablespoons achiote oil
1 tablespoon butter
1 branch of white onion, minced
2 ½ liters of water
2 cups of diced picadito
¼ of chopped cilantro

Preparation: Fry the achiote oil and the white onion. Add water and potatoes and boil for a few minutes. Add the noodles and cook until they are cooked. Add the milk and the cheese when the potatoes and the noodles are soft. Add the salt and butter and remove from the heat. Add the finely chopped parsley and serve.

MAIN DISHES

TUNA SOUP

Preparation time: 1 hour
Servings: 4
Ingredients:
A can of tuna 185 grams
2 cup chopped potatoes
3 cloves garlic
Salt to taste
Cilantro
Half cup noodles
Half a cup of peppers
Cumin
1 tablespoon achiote
Half cup finely chopped onion

Preparation: In a pot put the oil that came in the can of tuna, to make the sofrito. Then add the achiote, onion, crushed garlic, cumin, salt, pepper to taste and stir well. Add the bell pepper and chopped cilantro. While it is frying, add the potatoes and the corn and leave it for 3 minutes. Add the liter and a half of hot water so as not to stop the cooking. Add the noodles for 15 minutes, watching the pot because it can rise. After 15 minutes, check the potatoes and noodles.

Once ready, add chopped cilantro and serve.

RICE WITH TUNA

Preparation time: 1 hour
Servings: 4
Ingredients:
1 lb white rice
2 cans of tuna, 180 grams each
1 red onion (paiteña)
2 lettuce leaves
1 avocado
1 tomato
Salt and lemon to taste

Preparation:
Cook the white rice. Finely chop the tomato by removing the seeds and finely chop the onion. Dice the avocado and finely chop the lettuce.

Gather the tomato, onion, avocado and lettuce and add salt and lemon to taste. Mix the salad with the tuna. Serve the rice on a plate and place the salad mixed with the tuna on top.

RICE WITH CHICKEN ECUADORIAN STYLE

Preparation time: 2 hours
Servings: 6
Ingredients:
2 kg chicken breasts
2 cups uncooked rice
4 fried ripe plantains
1 onion in cubes
4 diced tomatoes
1 green bell pepper in cubes
2 carrots in cubes
1 cup peas
4 cloves of garlic
1 tablespoon achiote
1 tablespoon cumin
2 cups of water
Salt and pepper to taste

Preparation: Take the chicken breasts and season with a mixture made with all the spices listed. Place the chicken skin side down in a pan with hot oil and cook until golden brown. Add to the pan the onion, tomatoes, bell bell pepper and cook for about 15 minutes. Now add the water with the rice, peas and carrots and cook over medium heat until the rice is cooked. Serve the rice with chicken accompanied with fried ripe plantains.

BOLLO DE PESCADO

Preparation time: 2 hours
Portions: 10
Ingredients:
1 kg fish fillet (billfish, sea bass, albacore, mahi mahi mahi)
8 green plantains
4 tablespoons of oil or achiote
1 red onion
1 green bell pepper
4 crushed garlic cloves
2 tomatoes
3 subtle lemons
1 cup peanut paste
1 cup fish stock
2 cups of water
1 tablespoon finely chopped cilantro
Banana leaves for wrapping
Salt, pepper and cumin

Preparation: Peel and grate the green plantains without peel, add a little oil or achiote to prevent the dough from oxidizing. Finely chop the red onion and the bell bell pepper. Remove the skin and seeds from the tomatoes and dice them. Fry in oil or achiote with onion, garlic and bell pepper. Add the tomatoes and season with salt, pepper and cumin. Cook for 5 minutes and separate in 2 parts the sauce. Season the fish fillets with salt, pepper and the juice of the lemons. In a deep frying pan place part of the sauce with the fish fillets. Add 1/2 cup of peanut paste, cook for one minute and remove from heat. Cook the shredded greens with the remaining sauce. Add the water and the fish broth and stir constantly. Cook until a golden mass is obtained, add the remaining peanut paste and integrate the preparation until a homogeneous mixture that does not stick. Remove the pan from the heat and assemble the buns adding the cilantro. Spread the banana leaves on your work surface. Distribute the green dough and on top of it the refried fish, then wrap and take to a tamalera with boiling water. Cook for thirty minutes.

Add salt and lemon to taste. Serve with rice and onion curtido.

CAMARONES OR LANGOSTINOS AL AJILLO

Preparation time: 1 hour
Servings: 4
Ingredients:
1 kg of shrimps or prawns in shell
2 tablespoons butter or oil
4 cloves of garlic
½ cup white wine
¼ cup heavy cream
2 sprigs of parsley
Salt and pepper to taste

Preparation:
Melt the butter or heat the oil in a frying pan. Finely chop or crush the garlic and sauté in the pan for 1 minute. Add salt and pepper to taste to the shrimp or prawns. Add the shrimp and place them in the pan and let them cook on both sides. Add all the white wine and let it reduce by half. Add the cream and let it boil until the shrimps or prawns are tender. Sprinkle with finely chopped parsley. Serve the garlic shrimp with white rice, patacones and/or vegetable salad.

FISH CASSEROLE

Preparation time: 1 hour
Servings: 6
Ingredients:
1 lb of filleted fish (preferably corvina or mahi mahi mahi)
3 green plantains
½ lb peanut paste
2 tablespoon oil or achiote
2 red onions
2 chopped green peppers
2 tablespoons garlic
2 chopped tomatoes
1 tablespoon coriander, finely chopped
2 liters of fish broth or water
Salt, pepper and cumin to taste

Preparation:
Wash, peel and grate the green plantains adding a little oil or achiote to prevent oxidation. Finely dice the onions and finely chop the tomatoes and peppers. Fry the onions, peppers, garlic, tomatoes, salt, pepper and cumin in a frying pan with oil or achiote. Remove from heat and mix with 4 tablespoons of peanut paste and set aside. Cook the shredded verde in the fish stock or water and a little more than half of the refrito (season with salt, cumin and pepper). Add the remaining peanuts when boiling and leave for 30 minutes to cook the verde and blend the flavors. Stir constantly. Remove and add the chopped cilantro. Season the fish fillets with cumin, salt and pepper. In a casserole dish place a portion of the green plantain dough, arrange the fish fillets and add enough peanut sauce well spread and then add the last layer of green plantain. Bake in the oven at 350ºF until golden brown.

ECUADORIAN CHICKEN CHAULAFAN

Preparation time: 2 hours
Servings: 6
Ingredients:
1 liter of homemade chicken broth
1 kg shredded chicken
3 cups cooked white rice
4 tablespoons oil
1 onion
2 green onions
4 cloves of garlic
2 peppers
1 cup peas
2 carrots cut in cubes
6 eggs
7 tablespoons soy sauce
2 tablespoons Worcestershire sauce
3 tablespoons cilantro
2 tablespoons ground chili
1 teaspoon ground cumin
1 teaspoon of ground achiote
Salt to taste
Fresh parsley

Preparation: Start by heating the onion, garlic, sauces and spices in a wok. Cook until the onion is golden brown. Add the rice, chicken and diced peppers to the wok. Cook over medium heat for 10 minutes, making sure it does not stick. Make a stir fry with the eggs and add it to the wok together with the peas, the diced carrots and integrate well. Remove from heat and sprinkle with fresh parsley and onions for garnish. Serve hot in casseroles.

CHURRASCO

Preparation time: 2 hours
Servings: 4
Ingredients:
1 kilo of beef fillets
French Fries
Avocado
Tomato
Lettuce
Onion tanning
Egg
10 crushed garlic cloves
1 tablespoon ground cumin
Salt and pepper to taste

Preparation: Mix in a bowl the crushed garlic with the cumin, salt and pepper to prepare a rub for the meat. Rub the steaks with the rub and let them rest for a couple of hours. Grill or fry the steaks on the grill or in a frying pan on each side until cooked to taste. Depending on the temperature of the grill, this will only take a few minutes. Serve the churrasco with a fried egg on top of each steak and accompanied with rice, french fries, onion and tomato curtido, lettuce, avocado or chili.

ENCOCADO DE PESCADO

Preparation time: 2 hours
Servings: 5
Ingredients:
2 kg sea bass
1 white onion
2 red peppers
4 tomatoes
1 fresh coconut with its pulp and water
Juice of 2 lemons
Juice of 2 oranges
4 cloves of garlic
1 pinch of cumin
1 pinch of achiote
1 pinch of coriander
2 tablespoons oil
3 tablespoons fresh cilantro
Salt to taste

Preparation: Start by placing the fruit juice, garlic, salt and spices in a bowl. Prepare a sauce and paint abundantly the pieces of fish. Let stand for at least 4 hours in the refrigerator.

In a preheated pan with oil add the onion, tomatoes, peppers and salt to taste. Cook for a few minutes over low heat, add the liquefied coconut and cook for about 15 minutes more. Finally add the fish, and cook over low heat for 20 minutes more. Serve the fish encocado with the grated coconut and cilantro sprinkled on top and accompanied with rice and fried ripe plantains.

FRITADA DE CHANCHO

Preparation time: 2 hours
Servings: 5
Ingredients:
2 kilos of pork cut into medium-sized pieces (½ kg of ribs and 1½ kg of loin)
1 teaspoon ground cumin
10 cloves of garlic (5 whole and 5 crushed)
1 white onion cut into pieces
1 red onion
3 cups of water
1 cup orange juice
Salt and pepper to taste

Preparation: Season the pork with ground cumin, crushed garlic, salt and pepper. Let it rest in the refrigerator for a couple of hours. Place the pork, white and red onion, whole garlic cloves and water in a large skillet and cook until almost all the water is reduced. Add the orange juice and cook, stirring occasionally, until all the liquid is reduced and the meat is browned. Serve the fritada de chancho with yucca, mote, fried ripe plantains, onion curtido, avocado and aji criollo.

GUATITA

Preparation time: 2 hours
Servings: 8
Ingredients:
1 kilo of beef belly or tripe (well washed and cleaned)
Juice of 1 lemon
10 cups of water
5 sprigs of cilantro
8 crushed garlic cloves
2 teaspoon ground cumin
½ cup peanut butter
2 cups of milk
3 tablespoons butter
1 cup red onion, diced
2 cups of diced white onion
½ red or green bell pepper cut in cubes
1 peeled and seeded tomato cut into cubes
2 teaspoons of ground achiote
1 teaspoon dried oregano
4 peeled potatoes cut in cubes
Salt and pepper to taste

Preparation: Cover the tripe with water, salt and half of the lemon juice, let it rest for 10 minutes, wash it and repeat the process again. Wash it very well the second time. In a large pot, place the washed tripe with the 10 cups of water, the coriander sprigs, 4 cloves of garlic, a teaspoon of cumin and salt. Bring to a boil, reduce heat and simmer for 2 hours until the tripe is tender. Remove the belly from the water and let it cool a little, reserve 2 cups of the broth that was cooked. When the tripe has cooled, cut it into very small pieces. Place the butter, achiote, oregano, onion, bell bell pepper, tomato, cumin, remaining garlic and salt in a frying pan. Cook over medium heat for 5 minutes until the onions are soft. Separately, dilute the peanut butter with ½ cup of milk. Place this mixture in the blender with the refrito and the remaining milk. Blend until a creamy sauce is obtained.

Place the blended sauce, the 2 cups of tripe broth, the potatoes and the tripe in a large pot. Bring to a boil, reduce heat and simmer until the potatoes are soft and the liquid begins to thicken. Mash the potatoes a little to thicken the sauce and adjust the salt. Add pepper to taste. Serve the guatita with rice, pickled onions, tomato slices, avocado, and chili.

RICE AND LENTIL STEW

Preparation time: 1 hour
Servings: 4
Ingredients:
500 gr of lentils
3 tomatoes
1 liter of water
1 red onion
1 green bell pepper
4 cloves of garlic
A pinch of ground cumin
A pinch of ground annatto
A pinch of fresh coriander
3 tablespoons oil
Salt

Preparation:
In a large pot heat oil and add onion, bell bell pepper, tomato, garlic, spices and salt. Cook until the ingredients are tender. Add the liter of water and wait for it to boil, add the washed lentils and cook for one hour over low heat. Remove from heat and serve in individual plates accompanied with rice and fried ripe plantains, and fried chicken or meat.

CHICKEN WITH COCA-COLA SAUCE

Preparation time: 1 hour
Servings: 4
Ingredients:

8 chicken thighs with bone and skin
5 cloves of garlic
1 teaspoon ground cumin
1/8 teaspoon black pepper
2 cups of Coca-Cola
1 teaspoon salt
1 dash soy sauce

Preparation:
The first thing we are going to do is to make some holes in the chicken so that the homemade seasoning can get in. Then in a container we will make the dressing for the chicken: Add 5 cloves of garlic, 1 teaspoon of ground cumin, 1/8 teaspoon of black pepper, 1 teaspoon of salt and a little bit of water. This can be done in a mortar or in a blender. We grind well and the homemade dressing is ready. Then to the container where we have the chicken we will add a little mustard, a splash of soy sauce (a little bit to each piece) and the homemade dressing we prepared. Then repeat the procedure on the other side of the chicken. Mix everything very well.

In a frying pan add oil, let it heat and add the chicken pieces to fry a little. We let them seal for 7 minutes more or less and turn them to the other side. After searing on both sides, add 2 cups of Coca-Cola and half a cup of water. At this point we like to cook this step in an electric pressure cooker. So we remove the chicken from the pan and add it to the pressure cooker along with the coke and water. We cover it and put it in for 15 minutes.

If it is made in the pan, it is left for 25 minutes and with 1 cup of water. When it is ready, if we like it thicker, add ½ cup of water with 1 teaspoon of cornstarch and add it to the chicken and let it sauté for a while to thicken.

Once ready we can serve with rice and salad.

SANGO DE PESCADO

Preparation time: 1 hour
Servings: 8
Ingredients:

3 green plantains
1 tablespoon achiote
1 red onion
1 tomato
4 clove garlic
1 cup blended peanuts
1 lb fish (tuna fillet or mahi mahi)
2 sprigs of cilantro
¼ cup vegetable oil
Salt, pepper and cumin to taste

Preparation:

Peel and grate the raw greens, knead with achiote and a little water. Set aside. Prepare a refried mixture with the red onion, garlic and tomato. Add the refried mixture together with the liquefied peanuts, let it boil and add the previously grated and kneaded green beans, season with salt, pepper and cumin. Boil over low heat until the mixture is cooked and thickened. Add the fish cut in pieces, and the chopped coriander, let it cook for a few minutes. Add salt and pepper and serve with lime. It can also be served with rice.

SECO DE PESCADO

Preparation time: 1 hour
Servings: 6
Ingredients:

1 ½ kg chicken
8 tomatoes
2 green bell pepper
1 onion
3 cloves garlic
250 gr orange juice
1 cube of concentrated chicken broth
Fresh cilantro
Vegetable oil
Garlic powder
Sweet paprika
Ground cumin
Black pepper
Salt to taste

Preparation:
Sprinkle the chicken with the ground cumin, ground achiote, salt, and pepper. Blend the beer and orange juice with the tomato, onion, garlic, peppers, cilantro, parsley and oregano until a thick sauce is obtained.

Heat the oil in a large saucepan and add the pork chops. Brown on both sides and add the liquefied sauce. Wait until it comes to a boil and simmer for 1 hour until the prey is very soft, cooking time depends on whether it is chicken or hen meat.

If the chicken is tender but the sauce has not yet thickened, remove the chicken and cook the sauce over medium heat for about 10 minutes until thickened. Rectify salt and add orange juice to balance the bitter taste of the beer.

When the sauce is thickened, return the chicken to the pot and add some finely chopped parsley and cilantro. Serve the seco de pollo or chicken with yellow rice, fried ripe plantains, avocado, potatoes, salad, etc.

YAPINGACHO

Preparation time: 15 minutes
Servings: 4
Ingredients:

¼ cup Milk (60 milliliters)
1½ kilograms of potato
500 grams of cheese
¼ kilogram of Ground Peanuts
1 cup onion
1 sausage per diner
2 eggs per person
Cooked rice.

Preparation: Prepare a traditional mashed potato. Boil the potatoes with a little salt and mash them to the consistency of mashed potatoes, do not add any extra ingredients. Make potato balls and fill them with the crumbled cheese. You can use any white or fresh salted cheese. Flatten the dough with the cheese to form thick, flat tortillas.

Fry the potato tortillas in a pan with little oil, cook until golden brown on both sides and set aside. These tortillas are the yapingachos. Separately, make a sofrito with onion and butter. Cut the onion finely and when it starts to be transparent add the milk and the ground peanuts until it forms a thick sauce. Set aside. To serve the authentic Ecuadorian yapingachos, prepare the dish as follows: place the yapingachos on a bed of lettuce, on top of each tortilla serve a fried egg, place the previously prepared sauce on one side and on the other side your favorite sausages or chorizos. And a cup of rice per person.

DESSERTS

TROLICHES

Preparation time: 30 minutes
Servings: 8
Ingredients:

1 pound of sugar
2 tablespoons flour
1 liter of milk
cinnamon powder to taste.

Preparation: In a bowl bring the milk to a boil, mixed with the sugar and cinnamon. Separately, dissolve the flour in a little bit of milk and add it to the previous mixture when it starts to boil. Stir constantly so that the mixture does not stick, until you can see the bottom of the pot and check that the mixture has the necessary consistency to form the balls (Troliches). To proceed to shape them, take advantage when the mixture is still warm, because cold it hardens and it is impossible to mold it properly.

HUEVOS MOLLOS

Preparation time: 40 minutes
Portions: 12
Ingredients:

2 pounds of sugar
½ liter of milk
4 ounces of cookies
8 egg yolks
Cinnamon
Vanilla.

Preparation: Soak the cookies in the milk, add the sugar, dissolve it well, then add the 8 egg yolks, boil all this together with the cinnamon and vanilla until you notice that the balls can be made. Once the balls are ready, wrap them in tissue paper.

ECUADORIAN DULCE DE 3 LECHES

Preparation time: 2 hours
Portions: 12
Ingredients:

4 eggs
140 gr sugar
½ tablespoon vanilla essence
140 gr flour
For the liquid
1 can condensed milk
1 can evaporated milk
1 milk cream 500 grams
For whipped cream
1 sachet of whipped cream
1 cup cold milk

Preparation:
Start beating the eggs, sugar and vanilla for 8 minutes on high speed. Then add the previously sifted flour and mix with wrapping movements. Place in a previously floured and buttered mold until golden brown.
While it is cooking we make our mixture in a container with the three milks and stir well.
Then in the mixer add whipped cream, yeast and add a cup of fresh milk. We begin to mix at low speed and then high. For 4 minutes. Check that it forms peaks. And leave it in the refrigerator. Once the cake is ready, let it cool and add the liquid of the three milks, you can make holes in it with a toothpick so that it gets wet faster. Then decorate with our whipped cream mixture and the help of a piping bag.

TORTA DE MADURO

Preparation time: 2 hours
Servings: 6
Ingredients:

500 gr of wheat flour
5 ripe plantains
½ cup white cheese
50 gr butter
2 cups sugar
2 cups panela
5 eggs
2 teaspoons salt
½ cup water

Preparation:
Begin the preparation by whipping the butter with the sugar, then add two eggs and beat until a homogeneous mixture is obtained. Add the sifted flour and salt to the mixture and mix until a sandy dough is formed.

Place on the counter and stretch by hand, wrap in plastic wrap and keep in the refrigerator for at least 12 hours. Preheat the oven at medium temperature and in the meantime stretch the cold dough. Place in a springform pan and cover with aluminum foil.
After 10 minutes of baking remove the aluminum foil, and finish cooking until lightly browned, remove and let cool. In a saucepan place the panela and water and cook until a syrup is formed. Add the crushed maduros and caramelize them for half an hour.

Remove the mixture from the heat and let it cool, add the cheese and integrate. Pour the mixture over the pie crust, and bake at 160 C for 20 minutes.

Serve the cake with Ecuadorian black coffee.

PRISTIÑOS

Preparation time: 1 hour
Servings: 6
Ingredients:

2 cups flour
1 teaspoon baking powder
2 eggs
2 tablespoons butter
1 pinch of salt
½ cup milk
Oil
1 cinnamon stick
2 cups of grated panela
1 tablespoon lemon juice
2 cups of water

Preparation:

Place in a bowl the 2 cups of flour incorporating the butter, mix the eggs and the teaspoon of baking powder, add milk and the pinch of salt and knead until a homogeneous result is formed.

Roll out the dough with a rolling pin on a flat surface that is coated with flour, repeat the process until a thin dough is obtained. Cut the dough into a rectangular shape 15 cm long and 3 cm wide using a knife.

Form a circle with bangs facing outwards giving it the shape of a donut. Heat the oil in a slightly deep frying pan and carefully fry the pristiños, remove when they are completely golden brown.

Prepare the honey by placing the 2 cups of water with the grated panela, the cinnamon stick, the lemon juice in a small recipient, making the panela dissolve completely, carry out this process over low heat, and sift when ready. Serve the pristiños and bathe them in honey.

MAZAMORRA

Preparation time: 1 hour
Portions: 10
Ingredients:

4 cobs of hard corn
1 liter of milk
3 or 4 cinnamon sticks
Cloves
Sugar to taste
1 teaspoon vanilla essence
Cinnamon powder for decoration

Preparation:
Shuck the corn using a knife. Then blend (with a little milk) or grind to extract the juice from the corn.

Strain the juice and stir with the milk, place the corn juice in a pot and add the rest of the ingredients except for the vanilla and the cinnamon powder. Cook over medium heat, stirring continuously until it thickens. Finally, add the vanilla. Boil until the desired consistency is reached, then remove from the heat and let it cool a little.

Serve in individual containers and sprinkle with cinnamon powder.

SALCEDO ICE CREAM

Preparation time: 2 hours
Servings: 6
Ingredients:

Fresh fruit juice (blackberries, naranjilla, taxo, guanábana)
150 gr. cups of powdered milk
200 gr of milk cream
120 gr sugar
30 g of glucose
2 cups of water

Preparation:
In a blender, prepare a smoothie with the water, milk and cream. Take some of the previous preparation and mix it with the glucose.

Mix the glucose with the rest of the milk shake and the cream. Add the sugar and beat vigorously. Refrigerate for about two hours. Beat each fruit juice separately with part of the ice cream base.

In an ice cream mold, pour each portion of ice cream with fruits and freeze. Do the same procedure with the other fruits, alternating flavors and colors. Enjoy these delicious ice creams.

GUAGUAS DE PAN

Preparation time: 2 hours
Servings: 4
Ingredients:

5 gr dry yeast
1 tablespoon sugar
1 cup warm milk
1 kg flour
4 eggs
200 grams butter
1 cup sugar
Vanilla essence
1 pinch of salt
Choice of jam for filling

Preparation:

To begin preparing the leaven, add the yeast and sugar in a bowl, mix and add the milk, combine all the ingredients and cover with plastic wrap, leaving it to rest in a warm place for one hour.

For the dough, beat the eggs with the sugar, vanilla and pinch of salt. In a bowl place the flour and add the butter at room temperature, integrating everything with your hands.
Form a crown and add the beaten eggs and the leaven. Knead until the dough is elastic and let it rest covered with plastic wrap until it doubles in size.

Unmask the dough by stretching it on the counter and divide it into balls of about 100 grams. Stretch the buns forming rectangles, place the filling and roll up, the closure will be placed downwards. Shape the babies into heads, then brush with beaten egg and let rest for half an hour.

Bake in a preheated oven at 200 degrees for 15 minutes. Let cool and decorate with icing or chocolate chips.

COCONUT COOKIES

Preparation time: 2 hours
Servings: 8
Ingredients:

200 gr of grated coconut
100 gr butter
220 gr sugar
100 gr flour
½ teaspoon baking powder
1 egg

Preparation:
Sift the flour together with the baking powder. In a bowl, mix the butter with the sugar to a creamy consistency.

Add the egg and mix the ingredients well. Then add the grated coconut and flour. Refrigerate the mixture for a few hours before baking. Preheat the oven to about 360°F.

In a greased pan, place portions of the mixture and shape it into a flattened form. Bake for about 10 to 15 minutes until the edges are golden brown.

COCONUT FLAN

Preparation time: 1 hour
Portions: 10
Ingredients:

1¼ cup sugar
¼ cup water
2 cups condensed milk
2 cups of milk
4 eggs
1 cup shredded coconut

Preparation:
Heat the water and 1 cup of sugar in a small saucepan over high heat, bring to a boil and cook until the caramel begins to turn golden brown. Place the caramel in the mold where the flan will be prepared.

Blend the milk, condensed milk, eggs, ¼ cup sugar and grated coconut. Place the mixture in the mold with the caramel. Cook in a bain-marie over medium heat, covered, for 1 hour and a half until the mixture sets and remove from heat.

Let the flan cool in the refrigerator, remove from the mold and serve with grated coconut on top.

APLANCHADO

Preparation time: 2 hours
Servings: 3
Ingredients:

500 gr of wheat flour
50 gr butter
1 egg
2 egg yolks
2 cups powdered sugar
½ cup sugar
2 teaspoons baking powder
½ glass of orange juice
¼ cup oil
Vanilla essence

Preparation:
Start by mixing the flour, baking powder, salt and sugar, form a crown and place the egg, egg yolks, vanilla essence and butter in the center and integrate all the ingredients well.
Add the oil to the preparation, stirring constantly until a dough is formed, let it rest wrapped in butter paper for half an hour.

Roll out the dough with a wooden spoon until it is 5 mm thick and place it on a buttered plate. Cut squares of about 5 centimeters and bake at 180 degrees for about 15 minutes or until golden brown. Meanwhile mix the powdered sugar with the orange juice and form a glaze. Remove the squares from the oven and cover them with the glaze. Serve the aplanchados cold.

ARROZ CON LECHE

Preparation time: 1 hour
Portions: 10
Ingredients:

1 cup rice
2 cups of milk
½ cup sugar or panela
1 tablespoon vanilla
2 cinnamon sticks
½ can of condensed milk or 2 beaten eggs
½ cup raisins
5 cloves
2 tablespoons cinnamon powder for sprinkling

Preparation:
Wash the rice well and cook boiling for 20 minutes, until tender, stirring constantly.
Add the milk or beaten eggs, sugar, cloves and cinnamon.

Remove from the heat when the milk has the taste of cinnamon. Remove the cinnamon, cloves and peppers. Add the milk and raisins and boil for about 15 minutes more.

Serve hot or cold, garnished with cinnamon powder or cinnamon stick.

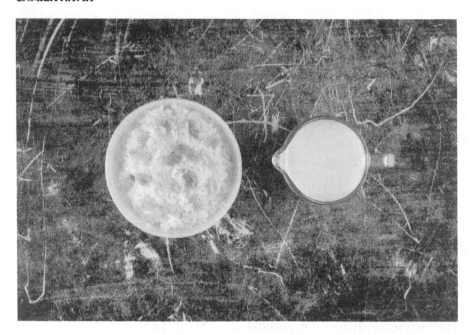

BREAD PUDDING

Preparation time: 30 minutes
Servings: 8
Ingredients:

10 loaves of salt bread (it doesn't matter if it is stale bread)
1 lb sugar (or to your liking)
1 liter of milk
3 eggs
1 glass of rum or brandy
3 tablespoons vanilla essence
½ lb melted butter
½ cup raisins (optional)

Preparation:
Place the bread and milk in a bowl, soak for a while and then crumble the bread until it is crumbled. Add sugar and let stand until dissolved.

Add the eggs, vanilla, liqueur and raisins. Beat with a wooden spoon until everything is well incorporated.

Add the melted butter and beat again vigorously. Pour the mixture into a previously buttered mold (it should not be more than halfway).
Bake the pudding in a preheated oven at 360ºF for one hour, or until golden brown.
Allow to cool before serving.

ENCOCADAS ESMERALDEÑAS

Preparation time: 2 hours
Servings: 8
Ingredients:

1 shredded coconut
2 cups of milk
½ kilo of grated panela
¼ kilo of sugar
4 egg yolks
2 ounces of butter
1 tablespoon lemon juice

Preparation:

Place the milk, panela and sugar in a saucepan. Cook over low heat, stirring constantly, until the sweet is thick. Add the coconut and bring to a boil. Add the butter and remove from heat.

Beat the egg yolks with the lemon juice and pour over the cocada. Return to the fire, continuing to whisk, until the candy comes out of the pot. Pour the mixture into a bowl and continue beating until it cools.

Form small balls, place on a tray and sprinkle with powdered sugar. Serve the cocadas cold.

FIG JAM WITH CHEESE

Preparation time: 2 hours
Servings: 3
Ingredients:

5 figs
1 cup cheese
3 cinnamon sticks
Cloves
1 cup panela

Preparation:

First cut off the tips of the figs so that they release the white liquid. We put them in a container with water for about 4 hours. Then we cook them in boiling water for approximately 40 minutes until they become small and soft.

Meanwhile we prepare the honey. For it we will use panela, water, cinnamon and cloves. We put it on the fire until the honey thickens. Once the figs are ready, drain them and soak them in the honey for 15 minutes. Take them out and serve with fresh cheese in strips.

ESPUMILLAS

Preparation time: 1 hour
Servings: 8
Ingredients:

8 ripe guavas
1 ½ cups sugar
2 egg whites
Blackberry syrup or sauce
Groats and/or shredded coconut

Preparation:
Peel the guavas, remove the center part with the seeds and place the pulp pieces in a large bowl, add the sugar, mix and mash until pureed.

Add the egg whites to the guava puree and sugar and use the electric mixer to beat the mixture until a creamy and firm texture is obtained.

Serve the espumilla immediately in ice cream cups or cones, accompanied with the blackberry sauce, gravel and shredded coconut.

BEVERAGES

RICE CHICHA

Preparation time: 2 hours
Servings: 4
Ingredients:

1 liter of milk
1 cup of rice, soaked one day in advance
½ liter of water
Sweet pepper
Ground cinnamon
Sweet cloves
Vanilla
Panela or sugar

Preparation:
In a pot we put half a liter of water. When the water boils, add the rice and the spices. Add: the cinnamon stick, the sweet peppers and the sweet cloves.
Stir for 25 minutes to prevent sticking. If you notice that the rice is drying out, add more water until the rice is cooked. Approximately 15 to 20 minutes.
The fire is turned off. Then remove the spices; the rice has already taken all the flavor and smell of the cinnamon, cloves and sweet pepper. Put the rice in a blender with the milk. First on low speed, then on high speed.

Strain all the rice through a strainer and return it to the pot for 10 minutes.

Then add the vanilla and the panela or sugar.
If desired, add a pinch of salt and nutmeg. Heat for 10 minutes and let it cool. Serve with enough crushed ice and ground cinnamon.

CANELAZO

Preparation time: 30 minutes
Servings: 5
Ingredients:

6 cups of water
8 cinnamon sticks
1 cup of grated sugar or grated panela
¼ cup brandy

Preparation:
Place the water, cinnamon and grated sugar or panela in a pot and bring to a boil.

Reduce the temperature and simmer, covered, for 40 minutes. Remove from the heat, add the brandy and serve the canelazo immediately.

CHICHA RESBALADERA

Preparation time: 30 minutes
Servings: 5
Ingredients:

¼ kilo of uncooked rice
3 tablespoons barley grain
8 cups of water
2 cinnamon sticks
8 cloves
8 sweet peppercorns (sweet)
6 cups of milk
1 can condensed milk
½ cup sugar
2 teaspoons vanilla essence
Nutmeg
Cinnamon powder

Preparation:
Wash the rice and barley in a colander. Place them in a glass bowl with 4 cups of water, cover and let stand overnight in a cool place (not in the refrigerator). The next day, blend everything, strain and place the liquid in a large pot.

Separately, place the other 4 cups of water, cinnamon sticks, sweet pepper and cloves in a saucepan and bring to a boil.
Add the blended mixture to the saucepan, bring to a boil, stirring constantly and wait until the mixture thickens. Remove from the heat, add the sugar, cold milk and condensed milk, and mix well. Serve the chicha resbaladera with ice cubes, sprinkled with ground cinnamon and nutmeg.

CHUCULA

Preparation time: 30 minutes
Servings: 6
Ingredients:

4 ripe plantains
2 cups brown sugar
2 cups of milk
1 teaspoon vanilla essence
1 glass of water
A cinnamon stick
4 tablespoons white cheese

Preparation:
Place the plantains, sugar, water and cinnamon in a saucepan and cook over low heat for 15 minutes.

Remove from the heat and blend with the milk, previously removing the cinnamon. Place the preparation in a saucepan, add the cheese and vanilla. Cook stirring constantly until it boils and remove from heat.

Serve well chilled.

OAT HORCHATA

Preparation time: 1 Hour
Servings: 2
Ingredients:

1 cup oatmeal
2 cups of water
2 cans evaporated milk
¾ cup sugar
1 cinnamon stick
2 teaspoons vanilla extract

Preparation:
Place the evaporated milk, cinnamon, Quaker oats, water, sugar and vanilla extract in a blender.

Blend very well until everything is well blended.
It is then strained to extract the cinnamon pieces.
Add crushed ice and serve chilled, garnished with more oat flakes.

MOROCHO

Preparation time: 1 Hour
Servings: 5
Ingredients:

2 cups of cracked brown corn kernels
6 cups of water
8 cups of milk
4 cinnamon sticks
½ cup grated sugar or grated panela
½ cup raisins
Ground cinnamon

Preparation:
Let the brown corn with the 6 cups of water soak overnight. The next day, strain the corn and place it in a pot with the 8 cups of milk.

Simmer for 3 hours, stirring occasionally, until the morocho is soft and tender. Add the sugar or panela, cinnamon sticks and raisins, and cook for about 20 minutes more, stirring frequently.

Serve the morocho hot, sprinkled with ground cinnamon.

MILK PUNCH WITH LIQUEUR

Preparation time: 30 minutes
Servings: 4
Ingredients:

½ liter of milk
2 eggs
1 cinnamon stick
1 glass of cognac (or to taste)
Sugar to taste

Preparation:
Boil the milk with the sugar and the cinnamon stick for about 10 minutes. Remove from the heat and let it cool.

In a bowl beat the eggs with a little cold milk and mix with the boiled milk. Beat everything until a foamy texture is obtained (preferably use a mixer).

Serve hot or cold adding a glass of cognac (or the amount you think convenient).

SANGRIA

Preparation time: 15 minutes
Servings: 5
Ingredients:

1 bottle of sweet red wine
3 oranges
2 green apples
1 can of peaches
½ peeled pineapple
2 peeled pears
2 tablespoons sugar
1 ice pack

Preparation:
Peel the apple, 1/2 pineapple, pears and cut into cubes, extract the juice from the 3 oranges.

Pour the wine into a pitcher and add the sugar, mix well until the sugar is completely dissolved. Add the orange juice and all the fruit to the wine. Add ice or keep refrigerated.

ROMPOPE

Preparation time: 2 Hours
Servings: 5
Ingredients:

4 cups of milk
6 egg yolks
½ cup brandy
1 cup sugar
1 teaspoon vanilla essence
5 sweet peppercorns (sweet peppercorns)
10 cloves
4 cinnamon sticks

Preparation:

Beat the five egg yolks in a bowl until they whiten. Set aside until later. Place 3 cups of milk with the cloves, sweet pepper and cinnamon in a saucepan and boil over medium heat for 15 minutes.

Remove from the heat and add the sugar. Mix well, cool in an ice bath and strain. Separately, slowly add the remaining cup of milk to the whipped egg yolk cream, mixing homogeneously.

Once the mixture is uniform, pour it into the boiled milk with spices and cook over low heat, stirring constantly, for 15 minutes until the mixture is slightly thickened.

Remove from heat and strain again. Add the vanilla essence and the brandy. Serve the cold rompope in a glass with a cinnamon stick (optional).